to: _Cynthia_

from: _Margie_

2014

There are only four kinds of people in the world —
those who have been caregivers, those who are currently caregivers,
those who will be caregivers, and those who will need caregivers.

Rosalynn Carter

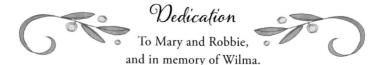

Dedication

To Mary and Robbie,
and in memory of Wilma.

Published by Sellers Publishing, Inc.
Copyright © 2014 Sellers Publishing, Inc.
illustrations copyright © 2014 Robin Pickens
All rights reserved.

Credits appear on page 64.

Sellers Publishing, Inc.
161 John Roberts Road, South Portland, Maine 04106
www.sellerspublishing.com • E-mail: rsp@rsvp.com
ISBN 13: 978-1-4162-4514-8

10 9 8 7 6 5 4 3 2 1

Printed and bound in China.

The Compassionate Heart♥

Caregivers Like You Make a Difference

Compiled by ROBIN HAYWOOD
Art by ROBIN PICKENS

SELLERS
PUBLISHING

Sometimes it helps
to know that
I just can't do it all.
One step at a time is
all that's possible —
even when those steps
are taken on the run.

Anne W. Schaef

Patience

priorities

Make your
own well-being the first
priority in your life.

Robin Norwood

Gifts

Self-compassion is simply giving the same kindness to ourselves that we would give to others.

Christopher Germer

Laughter and tears are both responses to frustration and exhaustion. I myself prefer to laugh, since there is less cleaning up to do afterward.

Kurt Vonnegut

Laughter

I have seen what
a laugh can do.
It can transform
almost unbearable tears
into something
bearable,
even hopeful.

Bob Hope

Keep your chin up.
No one expects you
to save the world;
otherwise you'd be
wearing a cape and tights.
Just do the best you can.

Doe Zantamata

Opportunity

Every challenge
has a gift for you
in its hands.

Richard Bach

Heroes are made by the paths they choose, not the powers they are graced with.

Brodi Ashton

Choice

Don't bury your vulnerability; learn how to use pain for the lessons it can teach. Be gentle with yourself. Take time to discover and enjoy pleasure.

Author unknown

Peace does not mean
to be in a place where there
is no noise, trouble, or hard work.
Peace means to be
in the midst of all those
things and still
be calm
in your
heart.

Author unknown

Calm

Benefit

Grow your faith, and you will
discover that there is
no longer the need to
have a sense of control,
that things will flow
as they will, and that you
will flow with them,
to your great delight
and benefit.

Emmanuel Teney

It's not the load that
breaks you down,
it's the way
you carry it.

Lena Horne

Spirit

Do what you can,
with what you have,
where you are.

Theodore Roosevelt

God's dream is that you and
I and all of us will realize
that we are family, that we are
made for togetherness,
for goodness, and
for compassion.

Desmond Tutu

Never believe that a
few caring people can't
change the world.
For indeed, that's
all who ever have.

Margaret Mead

One of the most vauable
things we can do to heal
one another is listen to
each other's stories.

Rebecca Falls

Listen

The miracle is this —
the more we share,
the more
we have.

Leonard Nimoy

My own heroes are
the dreamers, those
men and women who
tried to make the world
a better place than when
they found it, whether
in small ways or
great ones.

George R. R. Martin

Fearless

When you do nothing, you feel overwhelmed and powerless. But when you get involved, you feel the sense of hope and accomplishment that comes from knowing you are working to make things better.

Maya Angelou

You, yourself,
as much as anyone
in the entire universe,
deserve your love
and affection.

the Buddha

Remember

Try not to get
tired of doing
little things for others.
Sometimes, those little
things occupy the biggest
part of their heart.

Author unknown

No act of kindness is too small.
The gift of kindness may start as
a small ripple that over time can
turn into a tidal wave affecting
the lives of many.

Kevin Heath

Power

*Too often we
underestimate the power
of a touch, a smile,
a kind word, a listening ear,
an honest compliment, or the
smallest act of caring,
all of which have the
potential to turn a life around.*

Leo Buscaglia

You never know how strong you are until being strong is the only choice you have.

Author unknown

The most adventurous journey
to embark on is the journey
to yourself; the most exciting
thing to discover
is who you really are.

C. JoyBell C.

Accept yourself. Love yourself
as you are. You give a great gift to
the world when you do that. You give
others permission to do the same:
to love themselves.

Melodie Beattie

Begin

Don't wait until everything is just right. It will never be perfect. There will always be obstacles and less-than-perfect conditions. So what. Get started now. With each step you will grow stronger, more skilled, and more self-confident.

Mark Victor Hansen

Never be afraid to fall apart, because it is an opportunity to rebuild yourself the way you wish you had been all along.

Rae Smith

Vulnerable

Breathe

Your breathing is your greatest friend. Return to it in all your troubles, and you will find comfort and guidance.

the Buddha

Someday everything in your
life will make perfect sense.
So for now, laugh at the confusion,
smile through the tears, and remind
yourself that everything happens
for a reason.

Author unknown

Laugh

Credits:

p. 4 Anne W. Schaef; p. 7 Robin Norwood; p. 9 Christopher Germer, from *The Mindful Path to Self-Compassion: Freeing Yourself from Destructive Thoughts and Emotions*, 2009; p. 10 Kurt Vonnegut, from "Palm Sunday," a sermon delivered at St. Clement's Church, New York City; p. 13 Bob Hope; p. 14 Doe Zantamata; p. 17 Richard Bach; p. 18 Brodi Ashton, from *Evertrue: An Everneath Novel*, 2014; p. 21 Author unknown; p. 22 Author unknown; p. 25 Emmanuel Teney; p. 26 Lena Horne; p. 29 Theodore Roosevelt; p. 30 Desmond Tutu; p. 33 Margaret Mead, from *Curing Nuclear Madness* by Frank G. Sommers and Tana Dineen, 1984; p. 34 Rebecca Falls; p. 37 Leonard Nimoy; p. 38 George R. R. Martin; p. 41 Maya Angelou; p. 42 the Buddha; p. 45 Author unknown; p. 46 Kevin Heath; p. 49 Leo Buscaglia; p. 50 Author unknown; p. 53 C. JoyBell C.; p. 54 Melodie Beattie; p. 57 Mark Victor Hansen; p. 58 Rae Smith; p. 61 the Buddha; p. 62 Author unknown.